Ending the Israeli-Palestinian Conflict:

Arab-Jewish Partnerships

Other works by
Landrum Bolling

Search for Peace in the Middle East
(American Friends Service Committee, 1970)

The Future of Foundations: Some Reconsiderations
(Change Magazine Press, 1978)

Private Foreign Aid: U.S. Philanthropy for Relief and Development
(Westview Press, 1982)

Reporters Under Fire: U.S. Media Coverage of Conflicts in Lebanon and Central America
(Westview Press, 1985)

Searching for Peace in the Middle East [DVD]
(Foundation for Middle East Peace, 2006)

Ending the Israeli-Palestinian Conflict:
Arab-Jewish Partnerships

Landrum Bolling

Piedmont Press

Charlottesville, Virginia

Piedmont Press

Piedmont Press is an imprint of Just World Publishing, LLC.

All text in this work © 2014 Landrum Bolling.

All cartography © Just World Publishing, LLC.

All rights reserved. No part of this book may be reproduced or transmitted in any form or by any means, electronic or mechanical, including photocopy, recording, or any information storage retrieval system, without permission in writing from the publisher, except brief passages for review purposes.

Typesetting by Jane Sickon.
Cartography of Map 1 by Jane Sickon, 2014; Map 2 by Lewis Rector, 2010.

ISBN: 978-0-9845056-9-2
LCCN: 2014945597

Contents

Map 1: West Bank Fragmented by
         Israeli Settlements and Barrier.......... 6

Map 2: The Gaza Strip 7

Foreword by Ambassador Philip Wilcox, Jr. 9

Ending the Israeli-Palestinian Conflict........... 11

        Separation Barrier 26

        Gaza................................ 29

        Hamas and Operation Cast Lead 42

About the Author............................ 49

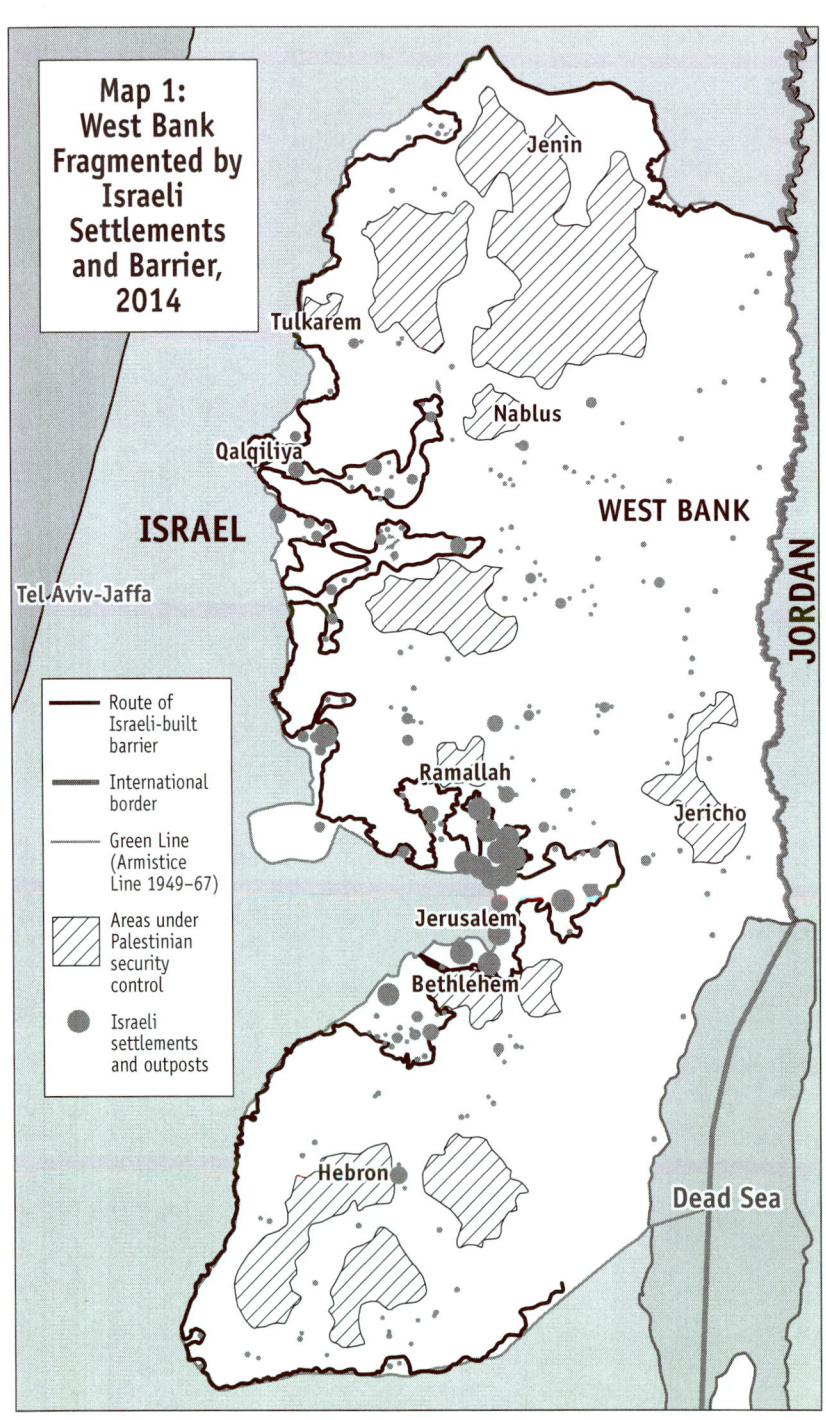

Cartography by Jane Sickon and ©2014 Just World Publishing, LLC.

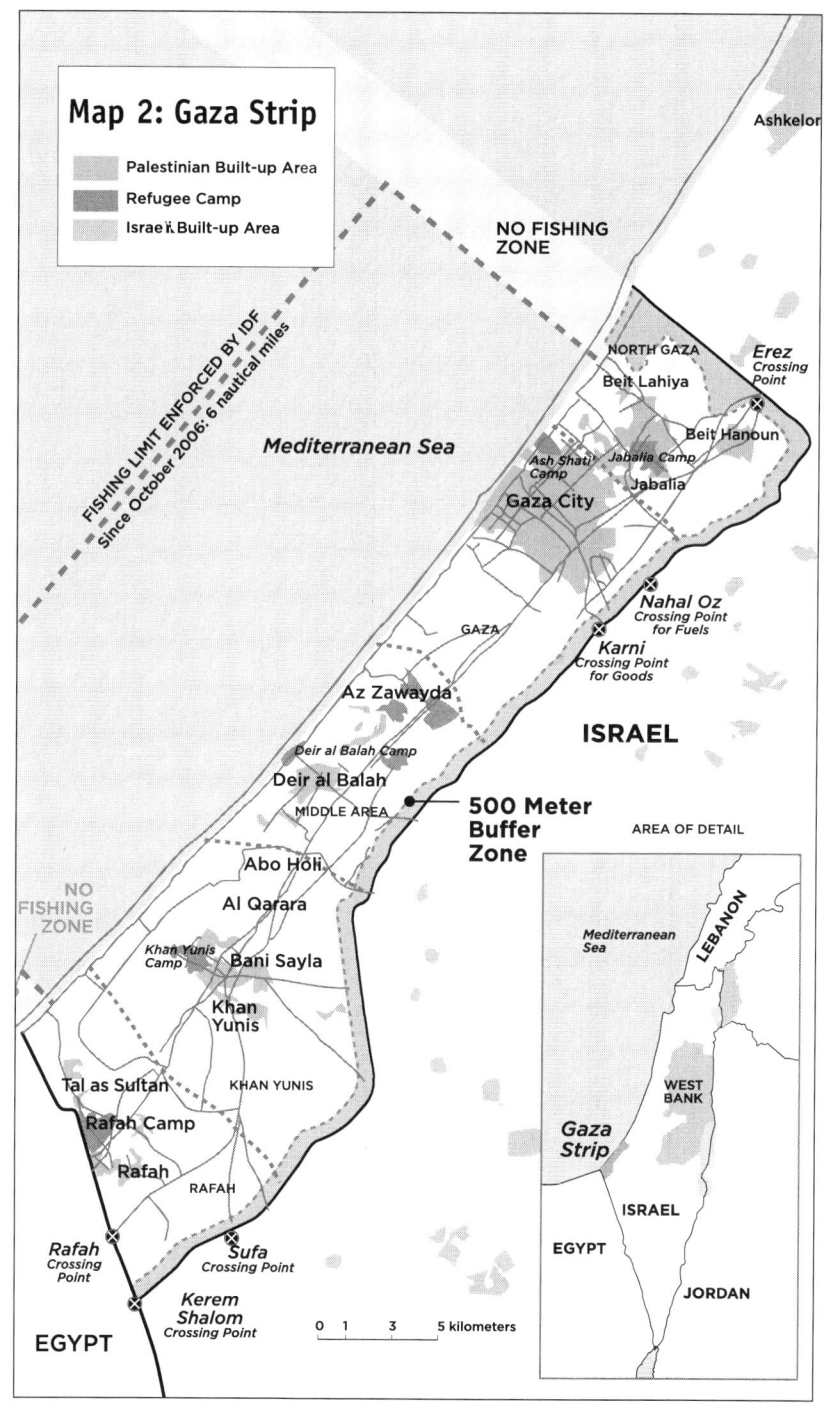

Cartography by Lewis Rector and © 2010 Just World Publishing, LLC.

Foreword

I know of no other American who can equal Landrum Bolling's forty years of commitment to and dedicated personal involvement in peace between Israelis and Palestinians. This brief book of deeply informed reflection and analysis is based on Bolling's unique and distinguished career as a citizen-peacemaker, a friend of and advisor to many American, Israeli and Palestinian statesmen, a philanthropic and humanitarian leader, and a constant advocate for a just Israel-Palestine peace. His efforts have touched the lives of many.

Bolling's book is a valuable review, beginning a century ago, of the competing struggles for nationhood, sovereignty, and security between Jews and Palestinians over the same land, to which both peoples are profoundly attached. In readable prose, it combines an efficient summary of diplomatic history with rich personal anecdotes that illustrate Bolling's analysis. The author's deep friendships with many leading Israeli and Palestinian activists and his respect and sympathy for the struggles of both peoples give this book special authenticity and credibility on a subject that, alas, has produced too much strident partisanship and too few prescriptions for peace.

Ending the Israeli-Palestinian Conflict breaks new and controversial ground on advocating a permanent solution to the conflict. It commands attention. For almost thirty years, the "two state solution" has been the goal of the United States and most other nations as the only way for Israelis and Palestinians to live together in peace. Bolling, once a supporter of the two state approach, now disagrees. He cites the utter failure of past diplomatic efforts to achieve a two state peace. He believes that separation of the two peoples, who are so demographically intertwined, and for whom close cooperation and interdependence are essential, has been proved unworkable, if not impossible, and, without a new way forward, will only produce further strife.

For Bolling, the alternatives—sometimes advocated by others, but seldom adequately analyzed—are a binational state or a Jewish-Palestinian federation. Either would require a major change in attitudes. But Bolling argues that close mutual cooperation in many areas, including economic, cultural, and governmental, will ultimately be embraced by both societies as they grasp the failure of the two-state separation model. Bolling acknowledges the difficulty of achieving this alternative. But as the Israeli-Palestinian conflict grows ever more dangerous, he urgently advocates that the two sides, perhaps initially at the citizen level, begin discussing and planning for this change. Landrum Bolling's vision of Israeli-Palestinian cooperation within some kind of entity that would enable such close cooperation is compelling as the ultimate destiny of both peoples. In any case, Bolling makes clear the urgent need for politicians and statesmen, and ordinary Israelis and Palestinians, to begin thinking more creatively about a more promising way out of this tragic conflict. Not least, the US government, which has in the past assumed the major foreign diplomatic role in Israel-Palestine peace, needs to rethink how it can be most useful and effective in helping Israelis and Palestinians make peace.

Ambassador Philip C. Wilcox, Jr.
Former President, Foundation for Middle East Peace
July 2014

Ending the Israeli-Palestinian Conflict:

Arab-Jewish Partnerships

The conflict between the Jews and the Arabs over control of the historic Holy Land has gone on far too long. For the sake of both communities and for the stability of the whole region, this conflict should be ended. Both of these gifted, hard-working peoples have inherited legitimate rights to live in the Holy Land. Almost certainly, Israelis and Palestinians (Christians, Jews and Muslims) will continue to co-exist in perpetuity, within that small sliver of Near East coastal lands between the Mediterranean Sea and the Jordan River. It is known as Eretz Ysrael (Land of Israel) to the Jews, and as Palestine to the Arabs.

Israel is well established as an independent sovereign state, with a strong economy and a powerful army developed over the past sixty-five years. It still has not declared what exact national boundaries it will ultimately claim for the Jewish homeland. However, the Israeli government has unilaterally decided to move hundreds of thousands of its citizens eastward from Jewish communities in Israel proper into new settlements in what has commonly been called the Arab West Bank. Meanwhile, the Palestinian Arab population has remained painfully divided. About 1.3 million Palestinians reside inside Israel and hold Israeli citizenship. About 1.6 million live in the Gaza Strip which has been controlled by Hamas (the Islamic Resistance Movement) for many years. Approximately 2.8 million other Palestinian Arabs live in Jerusalem or elsewhere in the West Bank—while millions more are forbidden by Israel from residing anywhere in the area that is their historic homeland, but are forced to live as refugees or in other forms of exile in other lands.

Since 1967, Israel has exercised political and military authority throughout the entire geographic area between the Jordan River and the Mediterranean Sea; the Palestinian Arabs living there have never been able to build a healthy independent economy, create a unified, effective political structure of their own, or to set up the Arab state they were promised more than sixty-six years ago. The long-term relationship between the two peoples is troublingly unstable and often tense.

Overshadowing all aspects of life for Palestinians today are their experiences as a conquered people under a foreign military occupation that has lasted since the end of Israel's overwhelmingly victorious Six-Day War of 1967.

Each side repeatedly blames the other as responsible for the long continuation of the conflict, characterized by the seemingly unending Israeli military occupation of the territories it seized in 1967. The leaders of each community have frequently expressed desires for peace, yet they have stubbornly reinforced demands the other side will not agree to. Mutual concessions for a compromise agreement have been virtually impossible to reach. However, over the years there has emerged an ambitious grand design for a comprehensive settlement that many (but not all) Middle East experts in the United States have labeled the "only" workable, mutually acceptable formulation for peace. This is known as the "Two State Solution." It calls for the division of the Holy Land into two states: a Jewish state of Israel, as has already been well established, and an Arab state of Palestine, yet to be created. This "two state" approach has been the definitive centerpiece of the Obama administration's initiative for Middle East peace. How realistic is it?

Could the decision-makers on both sides willingly accept this proposed deal? President Obama's secretary of state, John Kerry, tried to persuade them that they had no choice. Jewish and Arab leaders should not, he argued, "waste" more time in debates about the essential elements of the final peace agreement, which had supposedly been settled. Beginning in the summer of 2013, Secretary Kerry pursued an unrelenting campaign to bring the Palestinian and Israeli leaders into focused, uninterrupted, determined negotiations on the details for implementing the Two State Solution. A confident, hands-on mediator, Kerry issued explicit instructions to both sides. Their sole task now was to concentrate on working out provisions for proclaiming joint official acceptance of the Two State Solution and to arrange for its immediate implementation. No more delays. No needless arguments. This widely judged "only workable plan for peace" would now finally end the Palestinian-Israeli conflict—or so it was hoped. Increasing the sense of urgency, the negotiators were given a deadline: within nine months they were to have completed their entire assignment. By April 29, 2014, they should have put together a final draft of a peace treaty ready for signing. Kerry was lauded for his "courageous" unbending determination to prevent any further stalemates blocking peacemaking efforts. However, his success in getting new talks started did not carry over into attaining the agreement of the parties on the details of a peace. Serious differences persisted about substantive concessions each side would have to make to close a compromise deal. Before the nine months were up, Secretary Kerry had to downgrade his definition of what should be achieved by the late-April deadline— from delivery of a finished peace treaty draft to acceptance of an interim "Framework Agreement" that he presented, which would simply define the issues on which the negotiating teams would have to agree. This proposal, once again, required the division of pre-1948 Palestine into two independent sovereign states, Jewish and Arab.

    This arrangement has a long history. In the 1930s, Britain controlled the whole area west of the Jordan River, known as Palestine, under a Mandate from the League of Nations. British Mandate officials originated the plan for "Partition" of Palestine; and this proposal was endorsed by a royal commission sent out from London with the goal of ending, "once and for all", the troubles between Jews and Arabs. After intensive and prolonged consultations on the ground with all interested parties, the British authorities concluded that there was only one viable post-conflict arrangement the two sides could be persuaded to live with: division of Palestine between Jews and Arabs. However, each side immediately rejected the proposal. The dominant ambition and illusory hope of each community was that—somehow, someday—it could acquire sole control of all of the land. Neither side was willing to settle for merely a portion of a permanently divided Holy Land. Faced with the stubborn, aggressive opposition of both Jews and Arabs to the Partition Plan, the British dropped it. That was in 1937.

For ten years the idea was dead, but not forgotten. Meanwhile, World War II exploded. The world was forced to confront the unspeakable horrors of Hitler's campaign to exterminate the Jewish people. Global revulsion against the Holocaust inevitably intensified interest in the Holy Land as the refuge of choice for Jewish survivors. The future of Palestine continued to be a top-priority political and humanitarian concern for the post-war world.

World War II left Britain exhausted, economically depleted, and eager to start shedding the responsibilities of empire. In 1947, London dumped the responsibility for dealing with Palestine into the lap of the infant United Nations. Broad international involvement and fresh, reinvigorated ideas, it was hoped, could open the way to a new, generally acceptable formulation for resolving the Palestine Problem. But it was the old idea that won out. By majority vote in the General Assembly, on November 29, 1947, the United Nations adopted Resolution 181 that gave official international authorization for the creation, simultaneously, of the two long-proposed new states—one Arab and one Jewish. They were to be brought into existence following at least two months of preparatory counseling and facilitating assistance from the United Nations Special Committee on Palestine (UNSCOP). Detailed procedures were specified for drafting constitutions, preparing for elections, and setting up administrative departments—in accord with a UN schedule.

Within less than a year, the new state of Israel did become a reality. But not on the deliberately cautious UN timetable, nor with any of the stipulated consultative assistance to the Jews or the Arabs. No attempt was ever made to create the promised Arab state. Whether and in what form it might yet be accomplished remains a major perplexing issue for negotiators in 2014.

Today, even with the sustained attention and facilitation provided by Secretary Kerry's intervention, a comprehensive, mutually acceptable agreement between the Arabs and the Jews has continued to be an elusive objective. Incompatible policies, expectations and demands have endlessly frustrated peacemaking endeavors. Building mutual trust, developing working collaboration on common interests and needs, and nurturing a shared spirit of genuine reconciliation—these are indispensable requirements for a comprehensive, mutually satisfying and lasting peace. Such a peace, and not just the ending of violence and warfare, must be the ultimate compelling goal. Public renunciation of violence and confidence-building pledges of good will may be important symbols of the dawning of a new era in the relationships of old adversaries. But they are not enough. There need also to be practical works of mutually beneficial collaboration. Middle East peacemaking is a demanding, long-term "building project" type of undertaking. It cannot be accomplished quickly through only kind words or good intentions.

Peacemakers dealing with the Middle East conflict can and must learn from a thorough examination of past diplomacy efforts. What went wrong? And why? And, what should now be done? If the Two State Solution truly is the best "road to Middle East peace," why was it not taken long ago? And, if it still is the best option, what can be done to make sure it finally comes into being? These are inevitable questions, which will be addressed here.

Assessing its long troubled history, it must be recognized that at the heart of this conflict, from early on, is the history-shaping decision on the political future of the Middle East that the British government made shortly before the end of the First World War. On November 2, 1917, Foreign Minister Arthur James Balfour wrote a very brief letter informing the leadership of the Jewish communities in Britain and across the world that the British Cabinet, "in sympathy with the aspirations of the Zionist movement," had adopted a resolution declaring that "His Majesty's Government view with favor the establishment in Palestine of a national home for the Jewish people," and would take the necessary steps to achieve that objective. Thus did Britain make possible the realization of the extraordinary dream that the Viennese journalist Theodor Herzl had laid out in his little pamphlet entitled "The Jewish State," published in 1896. The pamphlet was both a vigorous indictment of European anti-Semitism and a stirring appeal for Jews to establish a state of their own.

The possible consequences of implementing the Balfour Declaration were debated from the beginning, and some of the most outspoken opponents were Jewish political leaders in Britain, including Lord Edwin Samuel Montagu, the country's only Jewish cabinet member. Moreover, an awkward, persistent problem was the seeming contradiction between the promises the British government had made to the Zionists and those made earlier to Arab leaders, who were demanding independent self-government in all the Arab-populated lands being liberated from Ottoman Turkish rule.

The text of the Declaration itself specified that nothing would be done that would adversely affect the "civil and religious rights of the non-Jewish population." It was not entirely clear what those rights were, nor how they would be guaranteed in an uncertain, changing political environment in which a sizeable Jewish population was about to be planted into the middle of the predominantly Muslim Arab world.

When World War I was over and won, Britain and their ally France were in firm control in areas of the Middle East that had been ruled for the previous four hundred years by the just-dismantled Ottoman Turkish Empire. The leaders of the Arab provinces of that empire had cooperated with the British troops in defeating the Turkish forces and had been rewarded with promises of independent self-rule, already in 1915. After the war ended, Britain retained direct administrative control of various districts of the region, including Palestine. With authorization from the newly born League of Nations, in 1922, the United Kingdom was granted a "Mandate" to rule over Palestine for an indeterminate period, with unrestricted authority, pending the judgment by the League's European-dominated leadership that the area's people were "ready" for self-government. At the time, the international Zionist leadership was begging for immediate permission to organize a massive immigration of Jews into Palestine and for expanded efforts to hasten the realization of the promised "national home for the Jewish people". The Arabs of Palestine (not surprisingly) feared that their long-term aspirations and interests were about to be undermined by British concessions to the Jews, who still made up a tiny proportion of the population of Palestine.

Britain was apparently caught in a trap of seemingly irreconcilable promises: to Zionist Jews and to independence-minded Arab nationalists. Undaunted by their dilemma, the British undertook to solve the problem by creating in Palestine a binational Legislative Council and administrative governance structures in which Jews and Arabs would share peacefully in powers and responsibilities. Possibly, under benign, democratic spirited British tutelage, a long-term resolution of the escalating conflict could have been worked out peacefully; but that did not happen. Both Jews and Arabs were filled with suspicions and hostilities toward each other. And neither trusted the British. Both developed well-armed, illegal underground militias that occasionally fought each other and, at times, took up arms separately against their British overlords. From 1936 through 1939, the Arab Palestinians mounted a widespread armed uprising against the British. During the latter months of that uprising, the British use of draconian countermeasures gave them the upper hand, and they were then able to disarm the Arab insurgents completely, but the Jewish underground organizations retained their weapons and their fighting capabilities.

During that Arab uprising, a royal commission was sent out from London to find a way to end once and for all the "troubles" in Palestine. After several months of investigation on the ground, the Peel Commission concluded that there was "only one possible solution": the partition of Palestine between Jews and Arabs. The immediate reaction from both sides was even wider, more violent protest. Neither would accept partition. The Partition Plan was soon abandoned by the British. In 1947, as mentioned, it was revived by the United Nations. But then, after the British forces left Palestine and the Jewish state of Israel came into existence, the Arab State envisaged by the United Nations never saw the light of day, and the idea of the Partition Plan fell into abeyance once again.

This time, it remained dormant until it was revived by international sponsorship in the 1990s under a new name: the Two State Solution. The old, long-ago-rejected idea of "Partition" amazingly re-emerged as the centerpiece of the celebrated "Peace Process" that took shape, with great acclaim and high hopes, after the famous handshake of the Palestine Liberation Organization (PLO) leader Yasser Arafat with Israeli prime minister Yitzhak Rabin on the White House lawn on September 13, 1993. Enshrined in the Oslo Peace Accords that were publicly signed that day, was the concept of "Partition," with the provision for a limited form of local self-government, called the Palestinian Authority (PA), to function in a portion of the occupied Palestinian territories, for an interim period pending the conclusion of a final-status peace agreement. This agreement was supposed to have been completely negotiated by May 1999 but it never happened.

The once enthusiastically proclaimed "Peace Process," unfortunately, turned out to be a great disillusioning disappointment. Angry, resentful Palestinians came to see it as a clever "Israeli maneuver" by which Yasser Arafat had been duped into accepting a so-called Palestinian Authority (PA) which never acquired any real credibility or authority, but instead, according to the widespread Palestinian view, served merely as a "sub-contractor" for carrying out certain functions of the Israeli occupation. (A high official of the PA once explained sarcastically to me, when I visited him at his office in Ramallah, that the government of Israel had granted to the PA "two major responsibilities: one, the collecting of garbage and, two, providing Palestinian security forces to protect the illegal Jewish settlements in the Arab West Bank." Neither of these assignments, he thought, contributed to better relations between Jews and Arabs, or advanced the "Peace Process.")

A revealing critical appraisal of the peacemaking endeavors of that era was publicly expressed in 2013 by Yossi Beilin, a veteran Israeli Knesset and former cabinet member who had helped draft the Oslo Peace Accords. He denounced his Israeli government's peacemaking efforts as a "farce." He also publicly advised Mahmoud Abbas, president of the Palestinian Authority, to dissolve his impotent pseudo-government, forget about the so-called "Peace Process" and turn over full responsibility for the Palestinians to the government of Israel. This was not an expression of support for the Two State Solution! It was, instead, a tacit acknowledgment that some other arrangement would have to be developed—even if nobody seemed to have any idea what that better alternative could be.

Despite all the negative assessments made of it, the Two State Solution continued to claim extensive stubborn support, year after year—from many Middle East specialists, diplomats and peace activists, especially in the United States. The claim persisted that this was the "only practical option" on the table, the only proposal widely endorsed by leaders of the international community. Accordingly, it would still have to be taken seriously by both Arab and Jewish peace negotiators.

Most important of all: from the beginning of the Obama administration's peace initiative, the Two State Solution was at the heart of the diplomacy pursued by President Obama and of the proposals developed by Secretary Kerry. As Kerry brought together the top negotiators for each side, he made it clear that their task was to work out the details for implementing the Two State Solution—and to accomplish that within nine months. The Palestinians and Israelis, of course, could not reject out of hand that demand from such an important international power. But they couldn't fulfill it either. The imposed deadline simply could not be met. And it was not.

Putting that disappointment aside, certain oft-repeated critical questions have continued to dominate efforts to define the issues:

- ◆ What are the reasons why the Two State Solution was not accepted and implemented earlier?
- ◆ What realistic expectation can there be for its acceptance now—or ever?
- ◆ What should be the essential relationships of the two states, if or when they both might be set up and functioning?

◆ What policies, program activities and operational procedures must be addressed for effective implementation of the hoped-for Two State Solution?

Many close observers of the Middle East conflict, including some Israelis, some Americans, and many Palestinians, have concluded that the Two State Solution is no longer viable or credible--not even a remote possibility. The reason? Primarily, they point to the ever-continuing expansion of the Jewish-Israeli settlement project in East Jerusalem and throughout the West Bank. More than any other single factor, these continuing settlement activities have undermined hopes for an outcome involving two states established in two distinct areas. Accordingly, it is argued, the Two State Solution had become unworkable and other options should be seriously explored.

The case against the Two State Solution , its critics declare, is based upon harsh inescapable realities. Those realities are commonly referred to by both Israelis and Palestinians, among both the general public and responsible officials, as "facts on the ground." These are the programs and policies, the established rules and regulations, the day-to-day operations of the Israeli occupation forces that control the daily lives of the Palestinians— and ceaselessly expand the West Bank settlements.

Critics of this vast undertaking, including some Israelis, insist that the prime purpose of the Jewish settlements, from the beginning, has been to make it impossible to create a viable Arab state within the bounds of historical Palestine. As more and more land in the West Bank, including crucially, in Jerusalem, has been swallowed up for the Jewish settlements, it has become increasingly clear that it is virtually impossible to patch together enough contiguous Arab lands to form anything that could be a viable, independent state. Moreover, powerful political voices within Israel have continued to oppose "the very idea" of a Palestinian Arab state. These voices have become ever more dominant in Israeli discourse since 1977, when the Likud Party first gained control of the Israeli government. The establishment of an Arab state, Likud declared then, must never be allowed "under any circumstance." When the Israeli government came under the leadership of Prime

Minister Benjamin Netanyahu he expressed openly his long time opposition to the Two State Solution. Under obvious American pressure, he finally gave a very grudging endorsement. But the "facts on the ground" of his policy of continued expansion of the settlement-building project meanwhile continued to undercut the possibility of the proposal being implemented.

Many people argue that the tenacious opposition of many Israelis, in leadership roles as well as within the population generally, is the real explanation for why the Two State Solution was not accepted and implemented long ago. The Israelis have simply never wanted it. And do not want it now.

Always, it must be remembered, the top Israeli political concern is "national security." Accordingly, many (probably most) Israelis regard any proposed Arab state within the Holy Land as an unacceptable threat to Israel's vital interests, even its survival. That widely held Israeli conviction naturally bolsters doubts about the wisdom and practicality of a Two State Solution.

On the Arab side, there is a strong desire for an independent Palestinian state—among Palestinians and among citizens and leaders of the existing Arab states. Statehood for the Palestinians is seen as essential to bring an end to the hated Israeli military occupation. It would also push forward the economic and political development of Palestinian society and foster reconciliation of the sectarian and ideological factions that have divided the Palestinian people.

The state of Israel currently controls all the land between the Mediterranean Sea and the Jordan River—and is the unmistakable economic and military superpower of the Middle East.

Currently, an important aspect of the Palestinian economy, including the paying of salaries for the PA bureaucracy, is its deep dependence on moneys controlled and disbursed by the US and the Israeli governments. Tax moneys collected from the Palestinians are held by the Israelis and transferred to Palestinian officials when and as the Israelis decide. This unhealthy relationship can be ended only by the emergence of a self-supporting, independent Palestinian state with its own national economy that enjoys direct links to the global economy, including the economic systems of its Arab neighbors. Today, among Palestinians there is, sadly, such deep distrust of the Israelis, that few Palestinians have much hope for genuine reconciliation with the Israelis—and no faith in promises about a "fair and just" negotiated two-state agreement.

Overshadowing every phase of Arab-Jewish inter-relationships are the Palestinian reactions to their daily experiences as a conquered people. The harsh realities of those experiences are commonly described by both Arabs and Israelis as "facts on the ground"—experiences that are the source of endless pessimism and hopelessness.

The impact of the assorted "facts" on the daily lives, the thinking, the feelings, and the behavior of the Palestinians—intensifying their despairing cynicism—can hardly be exaggerated. Pessimism is clearly one of the most powerful forces undermining the chances for peace, an inescapable effect of the "facts on the ground".

Consider these as chief among those "facts" that are recognized by both Israelis and Palestinians as damaging to the case for the Two State Solution, or any other plausible peace deal, are the following:

◆ Since Israel's victory in the Six-Day War of June 1967, approximately 600,000 Israeli Jews have come to live in Arab East Jerusalem and other parts of the West Bank, on lands long considered Palestinian. The investment that the Israeli government has made in this massive transfer of population totals many billions of dollars. It has evoked strong international condemnation. According to a ruling of the World Court, all these settlements are illegal—a violation of the Fourth Geneva Convention (to which Israel is a signatory) that forbids war victors to settle any of their civilian population on occupied lands. Israel's defensive rebuttal is that the West Bank is not "occupied" land but "disputed" land. That explanation raises another question: If the Israeli government has concluded that the West Bank territories are "disputed" lands —not "Arab properties"— will Israel now press its claim to full "ownership/control" of all the West Bank through eventual annexation?

- Of the total number of Israelis now living in the areas of mixed populations immediately bordering Jerusalem, about 200,000 reside in new modern multi-story apartment blocs constructed since 1967 inside or along the boundaries of East Jerusalem, where Palestinian Arabs have lived for many centuries, and where about 200,000 Palestinians live today. The recently constructed urban Jewish settlements are regarded by most Jewish Israelis as simply new or growing neighborhoods of their expanding Jewish capital city. Palestinians protest the continued proliferation and enlargement of what they call "illegal Jewish settlements within Arab East Jerusalem."
- Palestinians also denounce what they consider to be Israel's determined campaign to reduce the percentage of Palestinian Arabs in East Jerusalem and to expand its Jewish population so as to make all districts of Jerusalem more purely Jewish. This "Judaization" of Arab neighborhoods (as it is called) is seen by the Palestinian Arabs as a calculated effort to cut off Palestinian Jerusalemites from their compatriots and family members living in other parts of the West Bank —and, in time, to force them to leave.
- Palestinian Jerusalemites also protest the gross disparities in the per capita municipal investments made for the Palestinian areas of Jerusalem as contrasted with the much greater per capita expenditures for the Jewish-populated districts.
- Over the past half century, more than 400,000 Jewish Israelis have been moved into the more than 150 settlements established so far in various parts of the West Bank; with more being built all the while. These settlements are exclusively Jewish communities. Some of them are now small cities of more than 20,000 residents. Built and guarded under the watchful eyes of the Israeli Defense Forces (IDF), they have been constructed on lands taken from the Arab owners—or, in some cases, on so-called "public lands," thus classified by the Israeli authorities who have argued that they are thereby available for Israel to deal with as it likes. With the development of comprehensive urban facilities and services, shops

and factories, schools and hospitals, and even a university, these new communities are clear manifestations of major permanent changes in the physical and political landscape of the region. The idea that the Jewish settlements might eventually be dismantled or transferred to citizens of the long-promised Arab state is regarded by most Israelis and many Palestinians as an impossibility.

◆ In accordance with a comprehensive regional plan, these settlements have been linked together by a network of modern paved highways, most of which have been ruled off-limits to the region's Palestinians. The Arabs cite these so-called "Jews-only roads" as evidence that Israel is already acting as an Apartheid state.

◆ On higher ground in the central areas of the West Bank, as well as along the Jordan Valley, the Israelis have erected military installations that help to protect the settlements and guard against possible invasion from east of the Jordan River. (This, though Israel has had a full final peace agreement since 1994 with the Kingdom of Jordan, which lies to the east of the river.) At the end of 2013 the Israeli government announced that it was annexing the Jordan Valley and would keep troops on the western bank of the river.

◆ Over a period of several years, the Israelis have slowly carried out a policy of moving most of the Arab farmers out of the Jordan Valley, replacing them with Jewish settlers, on some of the richest agricultural lands in Palestine. More new Jewish settlements are being established in various parts of the Valley.

◆ Israel maintains many very permanent-looking military checkpoints deep inside the occupied West Bank and, on any given day, may supplement these with hundreds of additional "flying checkpoints" on the West Bank's long-existing Palestinian roads. Most of these checkpoints divide Palestinian cities and towns from each other, making normal trade and social intercourse extremely complicated, and sometimes quite impossible; only a small number of them sit astride the Green Line between Israel and the West Bank. At all these checkpoints, young Israeli military recruits control the movement of Palestinians from one place to another. Armed with their ever-present Uzis, they are instructed to check identity papers and travel documents and to turn back any persons they judge not to have appropriate official Israeli permits. Having to pass through these roadblocks, a twice-a-day time-wasting irritation and humiliation for many Arab workers, is widely resented as a particularly offensive form of subjugation to Israeli occupation forces.

The Separation Barrier

In the West Bank, over the years since 2003, the Israelis have finished most of the construction of a huge, 400-mile-long "separation barrier," part of which is a thirty-foot-high solid cement wall and part of which is long stretches of razor wire fencing. The stated purpose of the barrier has always been "to prevent the unauthorized entry" of Palestinian Arabs into areas populated by Israelis, including the illegal West Bank settlements. Since many of these settlements were built deep inside the West Bank, the Israelis built the barrier even deeper inside the West Bank, seizing additional large tracts of Palestinian land in order to do so. In protecting the illegal Jewish settlements, the barrier, in many places, cuts Palestinian communities off from each other. The International Court of Justice issued, in July 2004, a ruling that all sections of the barrier constructed inside the occupied West Bank are illegal under international law.

One highly conspicuous segment of the barrier is now encountered by all tourists and religious pilgrims who travel from Jerusalem to Bethlehem. The two historic cities are now separated by a massive steel and concrete wall, punctuated by watchtowers. These two sister communities and their holy sites have been linked to both Judaism and Christianity—and to each other—for two thousand years. The centers of the two cities lie only five miles apart, and there is less than a mile between their outer neighborhoods. The lives of Palestinian Christian families in Bethlehem and its neighboring towns were always tightly interwoven with those of their cousins, business partners, and staff colleagues in East Jerusalem. The barrier hampers normal working relationships that have existed for many generations.

A bypass road has now been built exclusively for Israeli citizens' yellow license-plated vehicles, enabling them to circle Bethlehem without entering it. Palestinians in Bethlehem are outraged that despite their continuing need to visit relatives and take care of business in Jerusalem—a ten- to twenty-minute drive away—they can now rarely go because of the hassle and humiliation of getting Israeli permits and passing through the control gate. Many are denied permits completely, with no reason given.

The justification for the "separation barrier," to many Israelis, is self-evident. "The barrier," some Israelis say, "has put an end to the infiltration of suicide bombers from Arab territories into Israel". The Palestinians respond by noting that suicide bombings stopped years ago, and that the total number of Israeli victims of suicide bombings—about one hundred over a ten-year period—was far smaller than the number of unarmed Palestinian civilians killed by Israeli soldiers and settlers in the same period.

Such arguments, of course, settle nothing in the fruitless, endless blame-game debates. Meanwhile, the Wall is a powerful, permanent-seeming symbol of the continuing and widening separation, suspicion, and hostility between the Arabs and the Jews of the Holy Land. The Wall isolates them from each other even more completely than ever. What is recorded

> above and in the sidebar is only a partial listing of some of the "facts" that define the Israeli occupation—and which, inevitably, undermine hopes for a peace agreement on the basis of the Two State Solution.

In the face of these realities, what reason can there be for expecting that a mutually acceptable two-state peace agreement could soon, or ever, be achieved? Is it conceivable that the Israeli government would ever evict from their homes and well-established communities several hundred thousand West Bank Jewish settlers—or any significant number of them—to make a viable Palestinian state possible? It seems most unlikely. As Israel's ambitious settlement-building program goes steadily forward—from one end of the West Bank to the other. It is generally believed that the Israeli government will continue to build new settlements and expand old ones into the indefinite future. The settlements provide desirable new home sites for Israel's expanding population. They are also widely (though not universally) judged by Israelis as making a valuable contribution to their country's overall national security.

Among Palestinians, however, the commonly held conclusion is that the settlements make it physically impossible for any mutually acceptable peace agreement to be reached that would allow a viable Arab state to come into existence. By its decision to build Jewish settlements on confiscated Arab lands, it is argued, the Israeli government has deliberately chosen a way to guarantee that there will be no possibility for a two-state peace agreement. The Israelis have repeatedly made it clear that they do not intend to cease construction of new settlements, or even to pause or delay the pace of settlement construction for any significant period. The settlements are permanent and an unmistakable hindrance to any efforts to implement the Two State Solution. Nevertheless, some earnest peace activists, including high-level politicians in the United States, have continued to urge Israeli and Palestinian officials to close a deal based on a two-state arrangement.

In July 2013, Secretary of State Kerry gave Israeli and Palestinian negotiators explicit instructions to join in concluding a two-state, final peace agreement "within nine months." He presumably believed that this request was reasonable, appropriate and doable. However, outspoken doubts about the wisdom and the feasibility of the Two State Solution have been increasingly expressed.

The *New York Times* on September 15, 2013, carried an arresting article titled "Two-State Illusion." Written by the highly respected scholar on Middle East affairs, Professor Ian S. Lustick of the University of Pennsylvania, its explicit thesis was: "The idea of a state for Palestinians and one for Israelis is a fantasy that blinds us and impedes progress." This challenge to the calculations behind the peace initiatives of the Obama administration was by no means new or unique. Despite the long history of support for the two-state arrangement, it never won conclusive acceptance. However, it was widely regarded as the most promising possibility for a deal that both Arab and Jewish publics and their leaders would accept. Moreover, there did not seem to be a better option.

Or was there? Is there now?

For a long time, I was a strong advocate of the two-state proposal. Indeed, I spoke and wrote extensively on its behalf—even during the lengthy period in which official US policy did not support in any way the establishment of a Palestinian state. My opinions developed out of the experiences I had traveling, studying, living and working in the region over a period of more than forty years. My views have been shaped by countless discussions with numerous friends—Israeli Jews, and Muslim and Christian Arabs —and through interviews and conversations I have been privileged to hold with top political leaders on all sides in various parts of the Middle East. Over recent years, however, as I have watched, up close, the unrelenting drive of the Israeli authorities to populate the West Bank with Jewish settlers, I have come to the inescapable, unwelcome conclusion that the two-state dream is now finished. The Israelis have killed it. Professor Lustick is correct in arguing that this "fantasy" should be put aside so that some more realistic, achievable solution might be designed and implemented.

> ## Gaza
>
> We cannot forget the vexing situation of the approximately 1.6 million Palestinians who live in the Gaza Strip. Around 80% of these people are families of the refugees from the war of 1948–49, whose claims to farms, properties, and homes inside the area taken over by Israel during those years have never been seriously addressed. One of the most overcrowded and impoverished places in the Middle East, Gaza has been under Israeli occupation rule since 1967.
>
> In 2005, Prime Minister Ariel Sharon withdrew from Gaza the eight thousand Israeli settlers then inside the Strip and the numerous soldiers deployed to guard them. The Israeli settlements in Gaza had long been a questionable security expense and a public relations embarrassment, with their attractive new homes, watered lawns, and swimming pools planted in the midst of the hundreds of thousands of wretched Palestinian refugees who live crammed into shabby camps, chronically short of both water and land.
>
> Sharon tried to portray his pullout of Israeli settlers and troops from Gaza as a beneficent, pro-peace gesture. But the Palestinians and other Arabs saw it differently. They argued that the settlements had been illegal all along, and that anyway, during thirty-plus years they had been in Gaza they had inflicted considerable harm on the Strip's Palestinians. Furthermore, even after 2005, Israel never gave up its dominance over Gaza. The Israeli military continued its firm hold on all the entrance and exit points between the Strip and the outside world, retaining its

> tight controls over the passage in and out of Gaza of both goods and people. (These controls completely contravened a formal "Agreement on Movement and Access," that Secretary of State Condoleezza Rice had personally negotiated in 2005.) The Israeli military also continued to manipulate the official population registry of Gaza, forbidding any non-Gaza-registered Palestinians from entering for any reason.
>
> Meanwhile, Israeli military activities in Gaza, of varying dimensions, have been a frequent occurrence since 2005; and on several occasions (most notably in 2008–9 and again in late 2012) Israel has launched large-scale military incursions into Gaza without suffering any significant consequences from international authorities.

Curiously, in the run-up to the establishment of the state of Israel there were casual discussions—but never a serious, concrete proposal—about a "confederation" arrangement that would link two semi-autonomous political entities, one Arab and one Jewish, into a single unified binational state. Long before Israel was created, two illustrious Jewish Zionist intellectuals had an even more radical idea. In the early 1920s, Rabbi Judah Magnes, the founder and first president of Hebrew University, teamed up with the famous Vienna-born philosopher-theologian, Martin Buber, in a campaign to achieve their vision of the Zionist dream through the creation in Palestine of a completely democratic, multinational state in which Jews, Muslims and Christians would have full, equal citizenship rights regardless of religion or ethnicity. They vigorously promoted this idea for several years; but they discovered, with great disappointment, that they could not sell the plan to most of their fellow Zionists, who were intent on creating a purely Jewish state.

Today, with indications of declining support for the two-state plan, there is a re-emergence of interest in some form of a binational, Jewish-Arab "one state" arrangement. In September 2012, a few hundred Jews, Christians, and Muslims gathered in Bethlehem to create an international, interfaith organization to promote the establishment in the Holy Land of a completely democratic state with equal citizenship rights for all residents regardless of religion, ethnicity, or presumed nationality. Thus far, this movement has not attracted much public support, but there is increasing debate on the two-state versus one-state issue. The true challenge is to formulate a solution that respects the singular interests and rights of both Jews and Arabs and, at the same time, promotes their partnership in areas of potential constructive collaboration. The one-state versus two-state argument is pointless.

History teaches us that, eventually, the most bitter bloody war can be and will be ended, one way or another. Various approaches have been proposed and employed in efforts to end wars over the long history of human conflicts. Not all may be relevant for efforts to bring the Israeli-Palestinian conflict to an end. Most wars are fought to a finish. One side or the other wins. And, then, the winning side imposes its will, its terms for peace, on the losing enemy. That historically conventional pattern, endlessly repeated through many bloody centuries, could well apply to Israel's numerous victorious wars. But significantly, it does not. The Israelis have fought and won five wars against the Arabs. Not one has led to peace with the Palestinians, though they were thoroughly defeated each time.

Over the years, Israel has developed a formidable ability to win wars. It has built a highly skilled, highly motivated, universal-conscript army (including women draftees, but exempting male religious-school students). Equipped with the best US military planes, Israel has acquired a most powerful, overwhelmingly effective air force. Of the highest importance, Israel has gained the undeviating support of the US military-political establishment, and is linked to the world's one military superpower more closely than could be provided by any formal military alliance. Israel receives each year many billions of dollars in economic and military assistance grants from the US government, covering a substantial portion of its annual military budget. Moreover, though they never talk about it, the Israelis possess an ample store of their own locally produced atomic bombs, accumulated despite international anti-proliferation agreements. In short, Israel is today the independent, undisputed military superpower of the Middle East.

Yet, despite its extraordinary victorious war record and its continuing massive armed strength, Israel has been unable to impose peace through its military dominance. Accordingly, that powerful "option"—winning a peace through victory in war —has so far simply not proved applicable to the Israeli-Palestinian conflict. If Israel should fight and win yet more wars against the Arabs, there is still no assurance that this would bring peace any closer.

Again and again, hopes for peace are raised with calls for more creative, more vigorous political interventions, more persistent, uninterrupted "negotiations." Repeatedly, the US government, at the highest level, has been drawn into playing a major role in promoting some kind of peace initiative. Consequently, the United States has been unrelenting in urging the leaders on both sides to keep talking to each other. After all these many years of Israeli-Palestinian discussions, debates and intermittent official "negotiations," the leaders and the general public on each side are well informed about the respective security policies, political ambitions, "red lines," vital interests, and bargaining positions that relate to this endlessly publicized conflict. There is no reason to believe that simply arranging more talks will bring peace—unless fresh ideas are introduced into the discussions. That, presumably, was what was intended to happen in the course of the Kerry-supervised negotiations. A predictable danger was that each side would cling to the conventional strategy of stubborn reiteration of fixed "positions." Inflexible desires and demands have to be modified or abandoned in favor of a joint exploration of shared "interests" and "needs." A peace of reconciliation must deliver benefits for both adversaries.

It must be recognized that a crucial challenge is to clarify just what a workable, mutually acceptable peace would look like. What would be its real purpose? The fundamental, essential purpose of any Middle East peace, of course, must be to put an end to violence between the Jews and the Arabs in Palestine. Here a serious philosophical and pragmatic political question comes to the fore. Will the peace that is so urgently needed be best attained and preserved by a strategy of separatism and mutually accepted isolation of Jews and Arabs from each other? Or would a genuine permanent peace be more securely established by shared, sustained working together for reconciliation and ongoing collaborative endeavors? Could two long-term adversaries enter whole-heartedly into close partnership activities? This is not an idle question. It is a serious issue of practical significance in the light of explicit policies adopted by the Israeli government. The "separation barrier" and the "Jews-only roads" are both unmistakable tangible evidences of a separatist strategy at work, a policy of minimizing contacts between Jews and Arabs in the hope that this will be the surest way to avert conflict. Whatever its possible short-range benefits, it cannot be an effective, reliable way to help bring about a comprehensive, lasting resolution of a deep-seated conflict. As inescapably close next-door neighbors, Israeli Jews and Palestinian Arabs are fated to live in virtually limitless, intense and intimate inter-relationships. How to make those relationships creative, mutually beneficial, and increasingly cordial—that is the real challenge, not how to keep Jews and Arabs "safely" apart.

What is here argued is that sustained joint efforts should be made by Israeli Jews and Palestinian Arabs to develop a broad assortment of practical working partnerships. Together, they should deliberately undertake to deal with a variety of issues and problems of obviously shared concern. Developing such partnerships could well be the most practical approach to ending the Arab-Jewish conflict.

(One of the most brilliant "elder statesmen" of the Zionist movement, the late Dr. Nahum Goldmann, a wise and much admired man I was privileged to know, once said to me something he also published widely: "The Jewish state will never have the true security it needs if it focuses on developing into 'Fortress Israel.' Ultimately, Israel's security depends not on building invincible defensive military power, but on cultivating true friendly cooperation with its neighbors.")

The Palestinian Arabs and the Israeli Jews will continue to be bound together on countless matters, large and small, into the far distant future. They cannot escape from one another, except by some form of ethnic cleansing. And that will not be allowed to happen. The Jews cannot get rid of all of the Arabs. The Arabs can't get rid of the Jews. Millions of Jews and millions of Arabs are fated to continue to co-exist within that small strip of land at the eastern edge of the Mediterranean. How they can best be linked together for peaceful collaboration—not how they can be kept apart by a "separation barrier"—that is the most important question. That is the most critical challenge to leadership on both sides.

An essential supplement to the ultimate peace agreement should be an explicit, shared commitment to work together on common problems, interests and mutual needs. Peace—serious, comprehensive, and permanent—will not come simply from the negotiation and public proclamation of a carefully crafted treaty document. Peacemaking between the Jews and the Arabs is a long-lasting building project, in which both sides must be fully engaged. The conscious aim on both sides in the resolving of all disputes should be to achieve "win-win" agreements—and to develop, wherever possible, compatible policies and programs for dealing with existing and prospective problems. Genuine peacemaking in the Middle East cannot be a "zero-sum game" directed toward a "winner-take-all" conclusion. Mutually beneficial, practical working partnerships should be the real goal.

Partnerships can, of course, be developed in a variety of fields: health care, crime prevention, suppression of drug and human trafficking, expansion and conservation of scarce water resources. On economic matters, among the most profitable opportunities for joint ventures and shared profits are available in the tourism industry, which is a powerful "engine" to drive the economies of both societies. In no other region on earth is there such a concentration of historical, archeological, and religious sites and monuments. Jews and Arabs have an exceedingly valuable stake in protecting, preserving, and developing tourist sites and services jointly throughout the region.

The administrative mechanisms for successful partnerships can, of course, take any of several different forms. A "federation," at one time, could have linked together Israel and Palestine on a broad or narrow designation of joint activities—and it was at one point vaguely talked about. Today the idea would be most unlikely to secure serious sponsorship. But governance structure and administrative relationships are not the central concern. What is most important is to cultivate attitudes, beliefs, and practices that encourage openness to collaboration in many endeavors—cultural, economic, social, and political. The possibilities are limitless, once people on both sides accept the concept of building peace through close collaboration rather than by trying to maximize separateness.

An impressive vision of what might have been achieved in a comprehensive Arab-Jewish partnership was laid out in detail in UN Resolution 181 of November 1947. That was the resolution that is usually called just the "Partition Plan." As noted above, it was never fully implemented—but it has also never been rescinded. The full title of the resolution was significant. As adopted by the Security Council in 1947 it was called the "Plan of Partition with Economic Union." Its principal provisions included this one:

The Economic Union of Palestine

The objectives of the Economic Union of Palestine shall be

a. A customs union;
b. A joint currency system providing for a single foreign exchange rate;
c. Operation in the common interest on a non-discriminatory basis of railways, inter-State highways; postal, telephone and telegraph services and ports and airports involved in international trade and commerce;
d. Joint economic development, especially in respect of irrigation, land reclamation and soil conservation;
e, Access for both states....on a non-discriminatory basis to water and power facilities.

Another section of the resolution, entitled "Freedom of Transit and Visit" called for "provisions preserving freedom of transit and visit for all residents or citizens of both states....subject to security considerations, provided that each State ...shall control residence within its borders." (No suggestion of a "separation barrier" there!)

Six months after the adoption of that resolution, the state of Israel was unilaterally proclaimed by a small group of Zionist leaders in Tel Aviv—but their action was not in accord with the procedures specified by the United Nations. Most of the Jews and Arabs in Palestine had opposed the Partition Plan when it was first passed by the United Nations. Indeed, the Arab Palestinians had publicly and emphatically rejected it. But David Ben-Gurion, who was the undisputed and most powerful leader of the Israeli Yishuv (Jewish community), and soon to be installed as Israel's first prime minister, convinced his Zionist colleagues to announce that they "accepted" the resolution. He had proposed a daring strategy based on his unique interpretation of the resolution and how to deal with it. Most of the provisions of Resolution 181 (the Partition Plan) could, he said, simply be ignored. The Jewish leadership did not need UN political advisors to assist them in setting up the new state. The only thing they wanted or needed from the UN was that very brief clause in the resolution that authorized the creation of a Jewish state (alongside an Arab state.) They had a virtual government already in place. They had no desire to operate railways, seaports, and airports jointly with the Arabs. They saw no advantage in shared programs for economic development. They definitely did not want an economic union with the proposed Arab state. They were strongly opposed to what they considered a too slow-moving timetable for the UN-facilitated formation of their Jewish state. Understandably, but regrettably, they took no interest in the creation of the Arab state called for in the UN resolution. Leaders of the Jewish community believed themselves to be fully authorized to proclaim the establishment of the state of Israel immediately, unilaterally, without even the ceremonial blessing of the UN. And this they did.

Within the same evening hours of May 14–15, 1948 in which the last contingent of British troops and administrators sailed for home, two dozen of the top local Zionist leaders met, almost secretly, in Tel Aviv. They read and signed together their declaration of independence, proclaiming the existence of the state of Israel. With no strings attached. With no recognition that an Arab state was to have been established at the very same time.

That, it might be said, was the end of the Two State Solution. If the letter of the law adopted by the UN had been honored and implemented, an Arab state and a Jewish state would have been established in 1948, on the very same day. Then and there, the Two State Solution would have become an official reality. That didn't happen.

If the Arabs had followed the example of the Jews and "accepted" the resolution, and if they had had a leader as tactically clever as Ben-Gurion, they, too, might have established a new Arab state that very same night, under the same claim that the UN had given legitimacy for the unilateral creation of new states, when and how their leaders might decide. The Israelis acquired their state at the earliest possible moment—and gained immediate official recognition from the United States and the Soviet Union. The Arabs, more than half a century later, still have not achieved their promised statehood. It remains to be seen whether they will now acquire that status through the US-brokered talks intended to implement, finally, the Two State Solution--or, by any other means.

The ultimate questions are about whether and how the two rival societies will be able to work out their separate but related destinies free of violence and destructive antagonisms. Is it possible that these two long-time bitter adversaries, their conflict rooted in ancient, ongoing animosities and cultural differences, can really break far enough out of the constraints of that conflict to create meaningful, positive relationships? Can they embrace the idea and take appropriate action to create a partnership in any field? Is there any credible evidence to support a rational hope for reconciliation and peaceful collaboration among Jews and Arabs?

There is. Over my past forty years of experiences with the peoples of the Middle East and their problems, I have concluded that the Israelis and Palestinians are surely two of the most creative, energetic, passionate, hospitable, resilient, and endurance-tested peoples on earth. And, at times, frustratingly stubborn. I know the communities well, admire them both and have many friends among them.

Let me offer an evaluation of their thinking and behavior related to the conflict and its possible solution, beginning by recalling some conversations I had long ago with the longtime head of the PLO, Yasser Arafat.

(There was a period during the presidency of Jimmy Carter when I served as an unofficial, unpaid, "easily deniable" courier carrying messages between the White House and Arafat. My primary mission was to convince Arafat about the wording of a public declaration he would have to make—recognizing the existence of Israel and renouncing violence—if he was ever to have any hope of talking with American officials about Middle East Peace.)

I remember saying to him one day: "You have been telling me for two years how much you want peace *if* only the Palestinian people could have a state of their own. But some Middle East experts say that a Palestinian state in the West Bank and Gaza, controlling only twenty-two percent of the land of Palestine, would be too small to have a viable economy. Would you be willing to have the Palestinians federated with, say, Jordan or Lebanon?"

"Yes, of course," he replied immediately. " But why not federated with Israel as well? We Palestinians should be federated with the Israelis."

On a later occasion, he brought up this subject – and gave it an unexpected twist:

"I don't understand our cousins" he began. (Arafat habitually referred to the Jews as 'our cousins.') "Why don't they understand what I see so clearly? Palestinians and Israelis ought to be partners. The Palestinians are the most highly educated, most advanced technically, most skilled entrepreneurs of all the Arabs. And the hardest working. Together, the Israelis and the Palestinians would build the strongest economy in the Middle East—a real force for stability, prosperity and peace."

I have no way of knowing how committed Arafat was to the ideas behind these fine words, or what practical steps he might ever have been willing, at some point, to take to translate them into action., These were unsolicited opinions that he expressed to

Ending the Israeli-Palestinian Conflict

me as his own. But, they were still only words, however honest they may or may not have been.

More significant are the actions of ordinary people that reflect their attitudes, hopes, fears, and serious intentions. I have been privileged, over many years now, to gain some understanding of the thinking, the feelings, and the behavior of a variety of Israelis and Palestinians. By observing and talking with them as they go about their daily lives, I have been cheered by what I have seen and heard of their working together in widely ranging locations and fields of common interests.

Halfway along one of the main highways from Tel Aviv to Jerusalem, but just off it, in sight of the ancient Latrun Monastery, there exists a modest binational kibbutz called Neve Shalom/Wahat as-Salaam, which its residents translate as "Oasis of Peace." About forty families, half Jewish, half Arab, have lived and worked together there for more than 25 years. Their children attend their small local school where they are taught in both Hebrew and Arabic. The community's main work and chief source of income is the operation of a small guest house. The residents also direct holiday camps for high school students, both Jewish and Arab, and conduct seminars on peacemaking for people of various age groups. They derive some income from guided tours of the region and from lectures about their work and life together. They also receive highly welcome donations from a variety of admiring individuals, groups, and foundations. It is a very modest way of life and they have embraced it with sustained enthusiasm. They are now in the process of expanding to a goal of sixty families.

There are numerous other, less intimate examples of cooperative endeavors by groups of Jews and Arabs. Particularly appealing and well supported have been projects in the arts: Jewish-Arab theater productions, documentary films for television and the social media, and various types of musical concerts.

One of the more noteworthy projects has been the Israeli-Palestinian Youth Orchestra. It was created by the joint efforts of a distinguished Palestinian-American academic scholar, the late Professor Edward Said, of Columbia University, and his close friend, the internationally renowned Jewish pianist-conductor,

Daniel Barenboim, who has served as musical director of several of the leading opera houses and symphony orchestras of major cities in Europe and America. They recruited the most talented young Palestinian and Israeli musicians, supervised their training to virtually professional level and sent them on concert tours in Europe and the United States. They proved to be a harmonious success in every sense of the word.

Of all the collaborative endeavors of Jews and Arabs, anywhere and in any kind of activity, none demonstrates so powerfully and effectively their commitment for peace as does the binational organization sometimes referred to as the Bereaved Families for Peace, sometimes called simply the Family Forum. The members are Jewish and Palestinian men and women who have lost a child or another close relative through a murderous act of violence from the other side. They meet regularly to exchange the stories of their painful experiences and their continuing emotional struggles to overcome anger, bitter feelings, and hatred—and to reinforce one another in working for reconciliation and peace. Their chief shared activity is giving speeches to high schools and other public audiences, both Jewish and Arab. Mostly, they go out in teams of two—one Arab and one Jew—to speak about the destructive futility of anger, obsessive resentment, and any desire for revenge. They emphasize the need for dialog among Jews and Arabs on many subjects and the possibilities for developing understanding and reconciliation in spite of the most grievous sufferings. Some of their discussions take on the political-military issues that underlie the conflict and provoke the violence.

One of the families whose tragedy drew them into this remarkable organization has been well known to me for more than 30 years. The patriarch of that family was the late General Matti Peled, a logistics genius who was the chief planner of Israel's fantastically successful Six-Day War of 1967. Immediately after that war, he quit the military and took his family to California where he earned a Ph.D. in Arab language and literature. Then he returned to Israel for a new career as a professor of Arabic studies at Tel Aviv University. More notably, he became one of the most highly respected leaders among Israeli peace activists and was elected to the parliament as an independent dove. (For many years he was my closest, most admired Israeli friend.) In a cruel irony, just two years after Peled's too-early death, his teenage granddaughter, Smadar, was killed by a pair of young Palestinian suicide bombers who blew themselves up on a busy shopping street in the heart of Jerusalem. Smadar's father, Rami Elhanan, and her mother, Nurit Peled Elhanan, had long been strong peace activists, worthy partners and heirs of the general. After their loss, they moved quickly to expand their peace promotion work through the activities of the Bereaved Families. They also intensified their efforts to build broad opposition to the continuing Israeli occupation, which they publicly blamed for the death of their daughter. A brother of Smadar, having completed his required military service in the Israeli army, joined other peace-minded young men, Israelis and Palestinians who had been fighters, in forming the binational "Combatants for Peace." Three generations within this one family have all vigorously struggled to advance the cause of peace—and to oppose various belligerent policies of their government. This is a quite remarkable family: Jewish, Israeli, heirs of one of the "elite" early Zionist leadership families—and fervently independent. But not unique. Many other Jewish Israeli families exhibit similar deep concern to end the conflict—and to work actively to bring about a permanent peace.

On my most recent trip to the Holy Land I had a startling conversation with a US-born rabbi, Jeremy Milgrom whom I have known for many years. Although he maintains ties with Jerusalem, most of the time he lives elsewhere—for reasons he frankly explained: "Thirty-five years ago," he said, " I came to Israel as an ardent young Zionist to help rebuild the Jewish homeland as a democratic Jewish state. Now, after all these years of turmoil, violence, wars, military occupation and ongoing hatred, I no longer believe in a Jewish state. We Jews do not need a Jewish state."

Avraham Burg is the son of a rabbi who founded one of the Israeli religious political parties and who, himself, rose in the ranks of the Israeli political system to become for a time Speaker of the Knesset. In 2010, he renounced his Israeli citizenship and wrote a book asserting that Zionism is no longer a positive, credible cause.

These developments are unmistakable signs not only of political dissidence in contemporary Israel, but also of an existential crisis in Zionism. Jewish liberals, within and outside Israel, take pains to insist that anti-Zionism is not a form of anti-Semitism but is consistent with traditional Jewish activism in support of human rights.

It is often said that Israel's long-evolving "peace camp" has been severely weakened by its inability to show more significant progress toward the ending of violence and the making of peace. There is weary disappointment among Israeli and Palestinian peace activists over the collapse of the so-called "Peace Process." There have been many expressions of concern that popular interest in peace is at a low ebb among Israelis. Hopes have been raised and dashed too often. Recurring acts of violence by both sides encourage that pessimism. People stuck in seemingly unending conflict situations can grow accustomed to a life of constant danger and learn to cope with fatalistic aplomb.

"Okay," say some Israelis, "so we don't have peace with the Palestinians, and have no idea of when and how we ever will. But we aren't doing too badly without peace. Our economy is strong and continuing to expand. In the field of information technology we are worthy rivals to Silicon Valley, with our own homegrown billionaires. Our agriculture is thriving. The tourism business, which for a time was crippled by fears of violence, is booming again. Despite the turmoil in some regions of the Arab Spring, we see no threats from our nearest neighbors. Our internal security problems are minimal. Things could be worse than our present condition of 'no peace and no war.'"

Hamas and Operation Cast Lead

In January 2006, Palestinians in the West Bank and Gaza voted in an internationally supervised election for the legislature of the Palestinian Authority (PA). The election was judged by international monitors as fair and honest—and Hamas (the Islamic Resistance Movement) won it. The more secular-nationalist Fateh movement that had long dominated the PA and the PLO had conducted a very chaotic campaign, and many voters were disillusioned by the Fateh people's record of graft and corruption. Overshadowing all other disappointments, the Palestinian voters were angry over the continuing land-grabbing by the Israelis for the unending expansions of their West Bank settlements—and the failure of the Fateh leaders to stop the land-grab or make any meaningful steps toward a just and lasting peace.

Hamas's election victory deeply alarmed the Israeli and US governments. US military advisers working with Fateh in Ramallah initiated a speedy effort to build a strong pro-Fateh security force in Gaza that could one day counter Hamas. But in 2007 the Hamas leaders, fearing just such a coup attempt, made a swift preemptive strike against Fateh's forces in Gaza. Hamas won a quick victory there, establishing the movement's full military and political dominance over all of Gaza.

Israel and the United States have long designated Hamas as a terrorist group. But in spring of 2008, the government of Israeli prime minister Ehud Olmert concluded an agreement with Hamas (indirectly negotiated through Egypt), for a six-month ceasefire between Gaza and Israel. The ceasefire largely held, but frayed toward the end of the six months—especially after Israel launched a significant military attack against Gaza in early November.

After the ceasefire's six-month term expired, efforts to negotiate a follow-up agreement failed. At the end of December 2008, Olmert's government unleashed a full-scale assault on Gaza by land, sea, and air under the ominous name 'Operation Cast Lead.' Its aim was either to directly unseat the Hamas leadership, or to inflict so much pain on Gaza's people that they would turn against Hamas. After three weeks of fierce fighting, the IDF had destroyed hundreds of factories, workshops, and farms, several schools (including the campus of the elite American School), and thousands of homes. It had also killed nearly 1,400 men, women, and children, a number that included perhaps two hundred Hamas fighters. When later I questioned a Gaza businessman (who detested Hamas's politics), he said: "The only thing the Israelis accomplished by their invasion was to strengthen the hold of Hamas over the lives of the people of Gaza—and to prove that the Israelis could and would perpetuate their blockade of Gaza and the wrecking of our economy."

Throughout Cast Lead, the IDF was unable to completely suppress the actions of those fighters from Hamas and allied groups who continued intermittently to fire their primitive rockets against civilian and military targets in Israel. (Israel's strict censorship always prohibits any reporting about rockets falling on military targets.) During Cast Lead, thirteen Israelis, including ten members of the IDF, lost their lives, and some communities in southern Israel saw daily life disrupted by the fear of rockets.

Finally, at around the time that Barack Obama was being sworn in as the first African-American president of the United States, Israel and Hamas concluded another ceasefire, and the Gaza-Israel border fell almost completely quiet. In late November 2012, another flare-up of hostilities between Israel and Hamas brought casualties and public denunciation to both sides—but once again, no glory or victory for either side.

The Two State Solution has often been called "the only road" to peace in the Middle East. It claims the firm backing of the governments of the United States and other major powers. It is ardently promoted by the leaders of the Palestinian Authority and by some Israeli and international peace groups. It may or may not be proved to the satisfaction of most outside observers that the Two State Solution is not a viable solution. But what other options are there? Answer: At least, a few.

Perhaps the oldest, certainly the hardiest, is the so-called "Jordanian Option." Its history takes us back to the year before the existence of the state of Israel was officially proclaimed.

In 1947 David Ben-Gurion, head of the Jewish community in the Holy Land (soon to be installed as Israel's first prime minister) sent Golda Meier on a highly secret mission. Disguised as an Arab woman, she travelled from Jerusalem down to the Jordan Valley to meet King Abdullah, the first ruler of what was then called the Hashemite Kingdom of Transjordan. Both knew that the first "official" Arab-Jewish war was just about to begin, but they both were prepared to make a *quid pro quo* deal. The Arab monarch, though bound to join other Arab leaders in declaring war, promised not to allow his well-trained Arab Legion to do anything to prevent the creation of a Jewish state—and specifically, that it would not permit Arab fighters to invade any of the territory the United Nations had designated for the new state of Israel. In return, the Israelis would allow Arab forces to move across the West Bank up to the edge of Jerusalem—with the understanding that the Kingdom of Transjordan could eventually annex the West Bank. The goals of the agreement were partially realized: The state of Israel was established, with all the land promised by the United Nations, plus a sizeable additional area gained by military conquest. The Jordanians ended up holding the West Bank, including the Old City of Jerusalem and the rest of the Eastern portion of Jerusalem. Soon after, the government of Jordan annexed the West Bank, but only Britain and Pakistan ever recognized that annexation; and in 1988 King Hussein renounced his kingdom's claim to the area. And so the West Bank remains a place of contention, still claimed by the Palestinian Arabs, but increasingly being swallowed up by the Israelis and their ever-expanding and illegal Jewish settlements.

It is a long, frustrating, sad and appalling story: the struggle, the endless disputations, the hostile intrigues, the recurring violent attacks, the murders, the assassinations, the wars. Surely, there must be some honorable way out of this morass of inter-communal rivalry, suspicion, hatred, individual and group violence, and war. There is: it is one that has been there ever since the United Nations voted its support for the "Plan of Partition with Economic Union."

All that may seem like ancient history. The ideas embodied in the Partition Plan may be dismissed today as unrealistic, idealistic, naïve—even quaint. All the same, it is worth recalling, not as a model for a new UN Resolution but as a reminder of the kind of spirit, the sort of vision that animated the designers of the "Two State Solution" that was proposed to the world, and officially endorsed, more than sixty-seven years ago.

Given the indecisive stalemate situation that prevails today, what credible judgment can be made about the real status of the Israeli-Palestinian conflict and its probable future?

Here is my summary appraisal of the situation:

- The Israeli-Palestinian conflict must be ended—and it can be ended.
- It will never be satisfactorily settled by total victory of the Israelis over the Arabs, even though the Israelis have overwhelming military superiority and an unbroken record of victories in war.
- Neither the Palestinian Arabs nor any combination of Israel's enemies will ever be able to destroy the Jewish state.
- Millions of Israeli Jews and millions of Palestinian Arabs will continue to co-exist in the Holy Land in perpetuity.
- Israel's military occupation control over the Palestinians, in operation for almost half a century, is exceedingly harmful to the national interests of both Israelis and Palestinians—and is unsustainable.

- Efforts to end the conflict between Jews and Arabs by building a "separation barrier" between them will not bring an enduring peace—at best, they will bring only a short-term truce.
- The hope for peace through the implementation of a Two State Solution is an appealing, popular, but now doomed, illusion. It will not happen.
- The goal for peacemaking endeavors must be not just to bring an end to warfare, but to establish a mutually beneficial, comprehensive agreement for sustainable peaceful collaboration.
- A workable, durable strategy for peace can best be developed and implemented through joint-action programs of governmental and non-governmental agencies of the Palestinian and Israeli communities.
- Serious, sustained attention should be given to creating and strengthening civil society institutions among both Israelis and Palestinians and to fostering practical ways of encouraging their collaboration.
- The Israeli and Palestinian political, religious, and educational leaders should make joint public declarations of their commitment to the building of permanent peace through appropriate "Arab-Jewish Partnerships" of individuals and organizations in both societies.

About the Author

Over the course of his long lifetime, Landrum Bolling has gained exceptional experience in international conflict resolution and in facilitating dialogue between members of different religions, cultures and ethnicities. His deep Quaker faith has shaped his life and work for peace and justice around the world.

Trained as a political scientist at the University of Tennessee and the University of Chicago, Bolling served on the faculties of Beloit College, Brown University and Earlham College, where he was president for fifteen years. He also served as president of the Lilly Endowment, one of the largest grant-making foundations in the world, and as chief executive officer of the Council on Foundations. Bolling was an Adjunct Professor in the Institute for the Study of Diplomacy at the Georgetown University School of Foreign Service. Bolling began his career in journalism, as a war correspondent in Europe during World War II, and has since written, co-authored, and edited numerous volumes.

Bolling's first book, *Search for Peace in the Middle East*, published by the American Friends Service Committee in 1970, initiated his lifelong quest to help bring about peace in the Holy Land between Israelis and Palestinians. In pursuit of this goal Bolling personally worked with many of the political and social leaders in the Middle East, met in the White House with President Nixon, and served as an unofficial interlocutor between President Carter and Yasser Arafat of the Palestinian Liberation Organization.

Bolling has worked extensively with Mercy Corps, an international humanitarian agency, as director-at-large and as a senior advisor since the 1980s. For three years Bolling was stationed in Sarajevo as the Mercy Corps representative in the Balkans. From 1983–88, he was the president and rector at the Tantur Ecumenical Institute in Jerusalem. He is also a senior advisor and board member of the Conflict Management Group in Cambridge, Massachusetts and a senior fellow at the Center for International Policy in Washington, D.C.

In recognition of his lifetime of work on behalf of international conflict resolution, Bolling has received more than thirty honorary doctorates from US and foreign universities. The University of Tennessee awarded him their prestigious Founders Medal in 1998. In 2000 he was honored, along with Senator George Mitchell, with a "Peacemaker/Peace Builder" award by the National Peace Foundation. Earlham College dedicated the Landrum Bolling Center for the Social Sciences and Interdisciplinary Studies in 2002. In 2005 Bolling received the CASE (Council for Advancement and Support of Education) award for his life of service to education. In 2008, the new Mercy Corps headquarters in Jerusalem was dedicated to Bolling.

Made in the USA
San Bernardino, CA
08 November 2014